MYTHICAL MONSTERS

The scariest creatures from legends, books, and movies

GENERAL EDITOR:

CHRIS MCNAB

tangerine press®

an imprint of

SCHOLASTIC

www.scholastic.com

an imprint of

SCHOLASTIC

www.scholastic.com

Scholastic and Tangerine Press and associated logos are trademarks
of Scholastic Inc.

Published by Tangerine Press, an imprint of Scholastic Inc.,
  557 Broadway; New York, NY 10012

Scholastic Canada
Markham, Ontario

Scholastic Australia Pty. Ltd.
Gosford, NSW

Scholastic New Zealand
Greenmount, Auckland

Scholastic UK
Coventry, Warwickshire

Grolier International
Makati City, Philippines

10 9 8 7 6 5 4 3 2 1

ISBN: 978-0-545-10972-7

Editorial and design by
Amber Books Ltd
Bradley's Close
74-77 White Lion Street
London N1 9PF
United Kingdom
www.amberbooks.co.uk

Project Editor: Sarah Uttridge
Design: Graham Curd

Printed in Singapore

Picture credits: All © IMP AB except the following: p32-35
© Amber Books Ltd.

Material previously published in *Mythical Monsters*

CONTENTS

INTRODUCTION

Godzilla

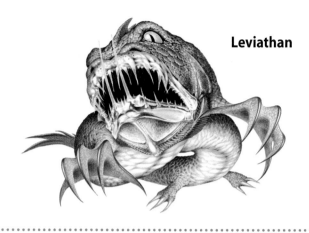

Leviathan

Dracula

For as long as humans have had fears, there have been stories about monsters. Some monsters were born of literature and myth—creatures such as Cyclops, the Sphinx, and the Basilisk. For ancient people, these were not mere fantasies, but real beliefs that haunted their lives. In North America, for example, Native Americans would tremble every time a storm slashed through the sky, believing that the Thunderbird was overhead shooting lightning bolts from its eyes and carrying storm clouds on its wings.

Legends of many ancient monsters often survived to terrorize people born hundreds of years later. The Basilisk, a lethal hybrid creature first described 2,000 years ago by the Roman writer Pliny, was still feared and encountered by the 16th century AD. In 1587, a Basilisk was said to have killed two young girls who were hiding in their cellar in Poland.

But haven't we moved on since then? Don't we know now that monsters are just products of fantasy? Don't be so sure. Several of the monsters in this book are certainly figures of pure invention. King Kong was created for cinema in 1933, and Godzilla has been a

Minotaur

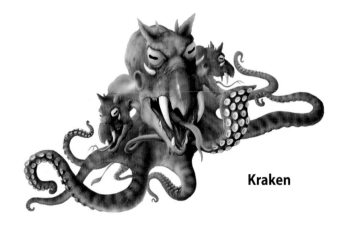

Kraken

Cyclops

Chupacabra

Loch Ness Monster

Bigfoot

star of film and print for more than 50 years. Yet, countless witnesses throughout history have claimed that monsters are every bit as real as you or me—they have seen them with their own eyes! Several hundred sightings of the ape-like creature Bigfoot have been reported in the USA and Canada. Scientists still aren't able to explain the huge footprints of the abominable snowman. More than 1,000 people claimed to witness the Jersey Devil in a single week in 1909—householders, policemen, and local officials say they came face-to-face with the terryfying beast.

All such monster stories lurk somewhere between fantasy and reality. Everyone knows that some creatures are pure myth; but people love to hear a good story! Oftentimes, skeptics discredit modern monster stories by giving scientific explanations—like Bigfoot is just a big ape. But what's so wrong with believing? Thousands of witnesses can't all be lying, right? Don't let the skeptics fool you. It's human nature to be interested in the unknown, and many people—even the nonbelievers—secretly want to believe in these strange beasts.

Gorgon

Mummy

King Kong

MUMMY

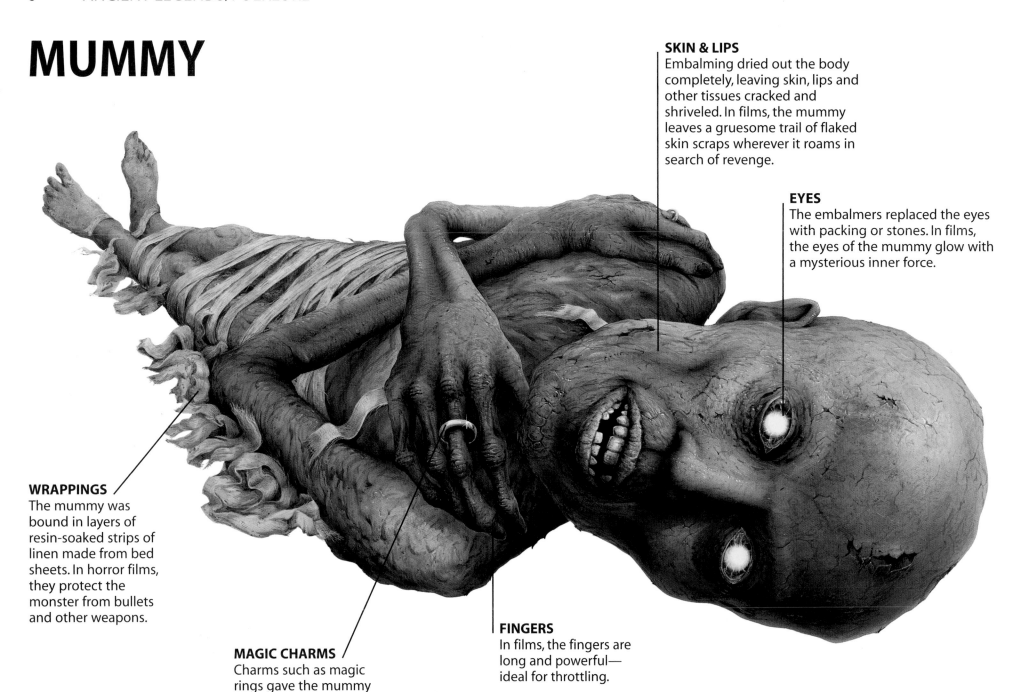

SKIN & LIPS
Embalming dried out the body completely, leaving skin, lips and other tissues cracked and shriveled. In films, the mummy leaves a gruesome trail of flaked skin scraps wherever it roams in search of revenge.

EYES
The embalmers replaced the eyes with packing or stones. In films, the eyes of the mummy glow with a mysterious inner force.

WRAPPINGS
The mummy was bound in layers of resin-soaked strips of linen made from bed sheets. In horror films, they protect the monster from bullets and other weapons.

MAGIC CHARMS
Charms such as magic rings gave the mummy great power.

FINGERS
In films, the fingers are long and powerful—ideal for throttling.

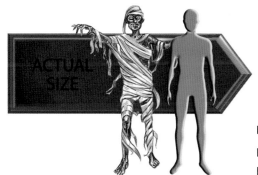

ACTUAL SIZE

Ancient Egyptians carved grim threats on the tombs of their embalmed kings, warning the living not to disturb the grave—or risk the wrath of the mummy... The mummy is an embalmed body that has survived intact in its secret tomb for thousands of years. Wrapped in strips of linen and sealed away with gold, jewels and other treasure, it is protected by a curse. In horror films, the mummy comes to life to take revenge on robbers and archaeologists who dare to invade its tomb.

Two archaeologists and their hired workers have spent weeks hacking at the rocks, and now the tomb's entrance is revealed. Also visible are the symbols spelling out a dire threat. The workers grow restless, but the archaeologists dismiss their fears. Using heavy axes, the workers rain blows on the entrance, which shatters with a deafening crack. Holding his blazing torch high, the lead archaeologist enters the tomb, with his colleague close behind. He looks around in awe as the torch's light glints off precious objects decorated with gold and jewels. A movement catches his eye and he turns to see a massive stone coffin open and a huge mummy appear. The mummy lumbers toward him with outstretched arms. Paralyzed with fear, the archaeologist stands helpless as he feels the mummy's powerful hands grip his throat—and begin to squeeze.

WHERE IN THE WORLD?

The best-known tombs of mummies are in the Valley of the Kings, in Egypt. The mummy of Tutankhamen still lies in his tomb here, near to the ancient cities of Thebes and Luxor, close to the River Nile. Other tombs were at Abydos, 93 miles (150km) farther downriver.

DID YOU KNOW?

● In medieval times, physicians often sold real or fake mummy's flesh and wrappings in powder form as a medicine. It was used to treat all disorders from acne to ulcers.

● Scientists set up the world's first international mummy tissue bank at Manchester Museum, UK, in the late 1990s. It holds tissue samples taken from mummies housed in museums around the world, for use in medical research.

● The Egyptian priests tried many different ways to protect the royal tombs, including inscribing bloodcurdling curses. They built huge granite doors and secret entrances.

CHUPACABRA

SPINES
These reportedly burst through the skin of the monster's head and back. Their purpose is unknown, but they may offer protection against enemies.

SIZE
Eyewitness accounts are muddled. Estimates of the creature's height in the standing position vary from 3ft 3in (1m) to 6ft 6in (2m) .

WINGS
The chupacabra is usually said to have bat-like wings with a span up to 13ft (4m). A few reports say it has no wings.

EYES
The size of hens' eggs, the big eyes glow an alien red. Some witnesses claim they fire laser beams to paralyze victims!

SKIN
Some witnesses say the beast has bare gray or blue skin, others that it has scales or fur.

CLAWS
The monster's feet and hands have huge, viciously curved and wickedly sharp claws for pinning down helpless prey.

LEGS
These are long and muscular for bounding 66ft (20m) at a stride when advancing on prey. Strangely, the monster never leaves footprints.

FANGS
Witnesses say the chupacabra's mouth bristles with great fangs. Some say they are bright red.

▷ A chupacabra swoops toward a small herd of goats and drops silently between the trees —a ragged silhouette against the night sky. Sensing danger, the goats shuffle nervously, then start to bleat in panic as the monster strides toward them, moving unnaturally fast on its long legs. Paralyzed by terror and the foul, sulfurous odor of the chupacabra, the goats are helpless to flee. The monster seizes the nearest one with its claws, plunges its huge fangs into the animal, and swiftly sucks out every last drop of blood. Goat after goat, it drains the whole herd, then slips off in search of other prey—for a chupacabra's craving for blood is never satisfied. It leaves no tracks behind.

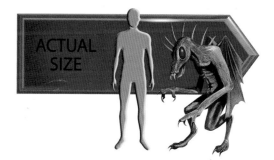

ACTUAL SIZE

A modern menace of the Americas, this blood-sucking, bat-like fiend is blamed by farmers and the authorities alike for the brutal slaughter of pets and livestock. This multi-fanged, many-spined, foul-smelling monster was first reported in 1995. It seeks out its victims in the dark of night and preys on a range of farm and domestic animals, sucking them dry of blood – its name means "goat-sucker," after its first victim. Some people say that the chupacabra comes from outer space, while others say it is the result of US military experiments.

WHERE IN THE WORLD?

The chupacabra is known in Central and South America. There are also reports from the southern states of the USA, including California, Arizona, Texas and Florida. Most sightings are from Puerto Rico, an island 994 miles (1600km) southeast of Florida.

Puerto Rico

DID YOU KNOW?

● Two Brazilian fishermen claim they shot a chupacabra dead and still have its head—which they refuse to let anyone examine.

● The mayor of Canovanas, a town in Puerto Rico, leads chupacabra search parties, armed with a crucifix and a gun. He also sets traps around the town in the hope of catching one of the elusive creatures.

● In 1996, a Mexican policeman opened fire on a chupacabra at close range—but his bullets had no effect, and the monster escaped.

● Attacks on humans are rare, but a nurse in Mexico reportedly lost an arm to the fangs of a chupacabra.

LEVIATHAN

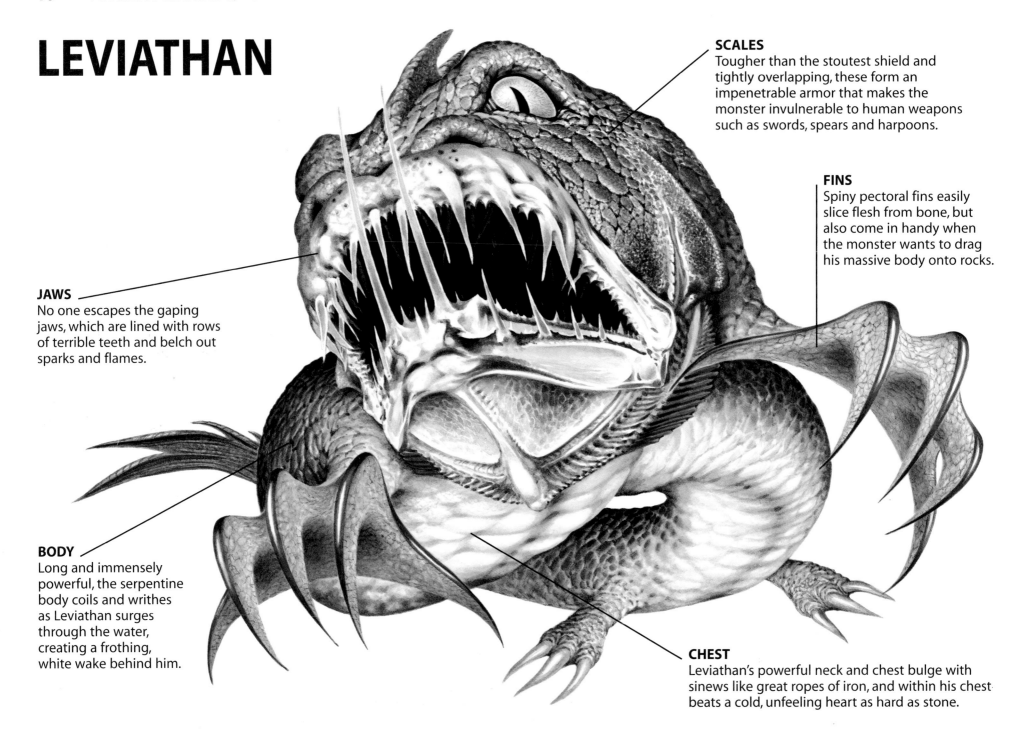

SCALES
Tougher than the stoutest shield and tightly overlapping, these form an impenetrable armor that makes the monster invulnerable to human weapons such as swords, spears and harpoons.

FINS
Spiny pectoral fins easily slice flesh from bone, but also come in handy when the monster wants to drag his massive body onto rocks.

JAWS
No one escapes the gaping jaws, which are lined with rows of terrible teeth and belch out sparks and flames.

BODY
Long and immensely powerful, the serpentine body coils and writhes as Leviathan surges through the water, creating a frothing, white wake behind him.

CHEST
Leviathan's powerful neck and chest bulge with sinews like great ropes of iron, and within his chest beats a cold, unfeeling heart as hard as stone.

Stirring up the ocean with his mighty tail, Leviathan creates a seething wall of water that gathers speed, bursts over the shore and completely overwhelms a small fishing village. Huts are shattered like matchwood and screaming victims are swept out to their deaths. A few locals escape the carnage by climbing trees, and they can only watch in horror as the monster rears out of the water to gloat at his handiwork and gobble up anyone washed out to sea.

ACTUAL SIZE

This primeval sea monster dominates the watery wastes of the world and has power over all the creatures of the ocean. He is chaos and evil personified, and he brings death and disaster in his foaming wake. His body stinks like a rotten carcass and he drinks the entire flow of rivers every day. His furnace-hot breath makes the sea boil, and when he sneezes, smoke billows from his nose. The Leviathan is first mentioned in Middle Eastern creation myths dating back more than 5000 years ago. According to Hebrew texts, Yahweh (God) made Leviathan and a female mate on the fifth day of Creation, but promptly killed the female to stop her producing offspring that might destabilize the world.

WHERE IN THE WORLD?

Leviathan has his origins in early Hebrew writings from the Middle East, dating back to about 3000 years BC. The Hebrews occupied Turkey, Syria, Jordan, Israel, Iraq and Iran—but the monster has the run of all the world's oceans.

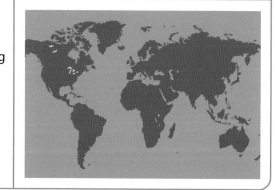

DID YOU KNOW?

● Early images of Leviathan from seal-stones and weapons show the monster with seven heads.

● Christians have identified Leviathan with Satan, with his huge mouth being the entrance to Hell.

● Most fish swim willingly into Leviathan's jaws, apart from the tiny stickleback. This he fears—for the stickleback was created to keep him in check.

SPHINX

WINGS
Huge wings carried the beast up to her mountaintop, from where she could survey the land and swoop down on people.

HEAD
The Sphinx had the head of a woman, with foul fangs to tear her victims limb from limb.

CLAWS
Wickedly long and sharp, these pinned victims to the ground and ripped open their skin.

TAIL
In many versions of the story the Sphinx had a snake for a tail. One bite from its venom-dripping fangs was enough to bring down even the strongest and most determined challenger.

FOREPAWS
The Sphinx held victims down with her huge clawed paws then crushed their windpipes with single massive bites.

HINDLEGS
These were powerfully muscled for leaping on to victims the moment they answered her riddle wrongly, giving them no chance whatsoever of fleeing to safety.

BODY
Some accounts say the Sphinx had the body of an enormous dog, but most describe it as being the body of a lioness in her prime. Whatever, it rippled with muscle built up from vast and regular meals of fresh human flesh.

High on Mount Phicium sits the Sphinx, guarding a narrow path. No one can pass unless they correctly answer her riddle—a puzzle taught to her by the Muses, the goddesses of the arts, and one she is sure no mortal man will ever figure out. Many brave men have tried: their bones litter the rocks around her den. Now, another intrepid traveler approaches. Nervously, he calls out: "Tell me your riddle, O mighty Sphinx." Fixing him with her steely gaze, the beast licks her lips then chants in a sing-song voice: "What walks with four legs in the morning, two at noon and three in the evening, and the more legs it has the weaker it be?" Trembling with fear, the man suggests "A grasshopper?" "WRONG!" screams the Sphinx and, before the man can escape, she pins him to the ground and clamps her teeth around his throat.

ACTUAL SIZE

This cruel monster of Greek legend challenged all who tried to pass her to solve a riddle—then slaughtered and devoured them when they got the answer wrong. The Sphinx was a horrible creature with the head of a woman, an eagle's wings, the body of a lioness and a snake for a tail, and she terrorized the poor people of Thebes in Greece from her domain on a mountaintop. She was finally killed by the Greek hero Oedipus, who marched straight up to the monster in her lair on Mount Phicium and demanded to hear her riddle. To her complete amazement, Oedipus answered confidently and correctly: "A man." Enraged, the Sphinx hurled herself off the mountain and fell screaming to her death in the valley below.

DID YOU KNOW?

● "Sphinx" means "strangler" and comes from the ancient Greek verb "sphingo," meaning "to throttle."

● Since it was carved over 4000 years ago, the Great Sphinx in Egypt has spent most of its time buried up to its neck in sand. The head has been badly worn by weathering and at some point lost its beard and nose. Also, troops of Emperor Napoléon Bonaparte (1769–1821) of France used it for target practice.

WHERE IN THE WORLD?

Depictions of Sphinxes are known from all over the eastern Mediterranean. In the Greek legend, the Sphinx came from Ethiopia and lived on Mount Phicium, which may be Mount Parnassus, in Thebes in Greece.

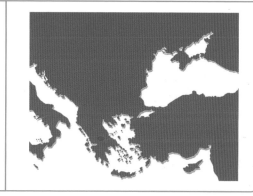

BASILISK

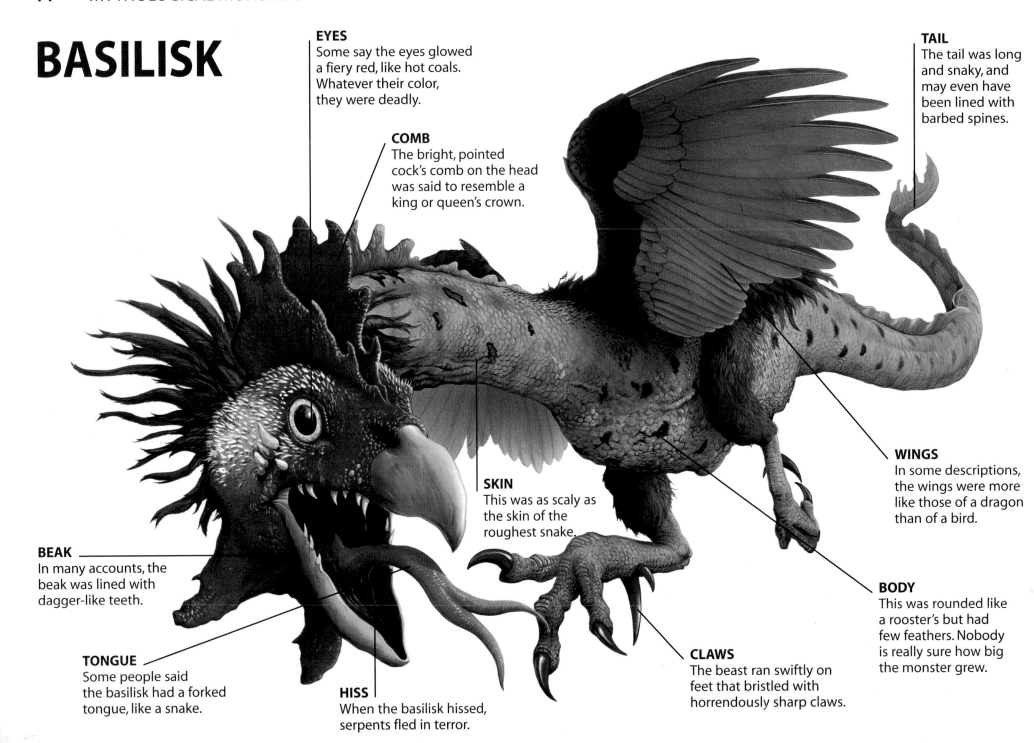

EYES
Some say the eyes glowed a fiery red, like hot coals. Whatever their color, they were deadly.

COMB
The bright, pointed cock's comb on the head was said to resemble a king or queen's crown.

TAIL
The tail was long and snaky, and may even have been lined with barbed spines.

BEAK
In many accounts, the beak was lined with dagger-like teeth.

TONGUE
Some people said the basilisk had a forked tongue, like a snake.

HISS
When the basilisk hissed, serpents fled in terror.

SKIN
This was as scaly as the skin of the roughest snake.

CLAWS
The beast ran swiftly on feet that bristled with horrendously sharp claws.

WINGS
In some descriptions, the wings were more like those of a dragon than of a bird.

BODY
This was rounded like a rooster's but had few feathers. Nobody is really sure how big the monster grew.

ACTUAL SIZE

▽ A fresh source of terror is about to emerge into the world. A toad has carefully tended a strange egg abandoned in a grassy field. The warty amphibian watches as first cracks, then a hole appear in the shell. Soon a bird-like head pops out—but this is no fluffy, harmless chick. Moments later, the toad keels over, stone-dead; it is the first victim of a new basilisk's deadly gaze.

The basilisk was a horrific mix of reptile and bird. It was said to be hatched from a freak egg laid by a cockerel, an egg that was then incubated by a toad. With their snake-like bodies, cockerel heads and stumpy wings, basilisks had terrifying magical powers. Just the stare of a basilisk could kill people, as could its foul poisonous breath. It polluted waterways and turned green, fertile farmland into nothing but barren desert. Rocks would shatter if the basilisk brushed against them. There were few ways to kill a basilisk. Weasels were said to be immune to basilisk magic and poison, and if a basilisk was confronted with a mirror, it would be killed by its own reflection.

WHERE IN THE WORLD?

The Roman writer Pliny described the basilisk nearly 2000 years ago, but the creature may be even older. People throughout Europe walked in terror of meeting it right up until the 16th century, when the famous naturalist Konrad Gesner denounced it as "gossip."

DID YOU KNOW?

● In Warsaw in Poland in 1587, a basilisk was blamed for killing two small girls in a cellar. Reportedly, a "volunteer" prisoner sent down into the cellar killed the creature with a mirror.

● The basilisk myth may come from early reports of hooded cobras, venomous Indian snakes that rear up and flare a hood of skin. The idea that a weasel can kill a basilisk may come from tales of the mongoose, a small mammal that preys on cobras.

CYCLOPS

HAIR
Sprouting wildly from the cyclops' head, the dirty, matted hair is infested with lice.

EYE
One huge, watchful eye stares from the center of the cyclops' forehead.

TEETH
When the cyclops wants a snack, he rips up humans with his big, pointed teeth.

ARMS
Bulging with muscles, the long arms pound out metal and shift stone blocks with ease.

CLAWS
Instead of nails, hooked claws grow from the fingers and toes. If the cyclops is in a bad mood, these make formidable weapons.

FEET
The whole ground shakes when the cyclops stamps around on his massive feet.

ACTUAL SIZE

▷ Odysseus waited patiently for the Cyclops to fall asleep. Then the hero sharpened a stake and heated it in the fire. Driving the weapon into the scary giant's eye, Odysseus twisted the stake around, blinding Polyphemus. The survivors escaped the next day, clinging to the bellies of the cyclops' sheep as he sent them out to graze.

The single eye of the cyclops stares menacingly from its horrible, hairy face. This cruel, watchful giant can smash a human to pieces with a single flick of the wrist. In Greek mythology, the first cyclopes were three brothers called Steropes, Brontes and Arges, sons of Ge (Mother Earth) and the god Uranus. They were blacksmiths by trade. The last race of cyclopes were brutish shepherds who lived squalid lives in dingy caves in Sicily, tending their flocks and tearing intruders apart. They communicated with grunts and roars. The cyclops Polyphemus was the most dreadful of all. When Odysseus and his men turned up at his cave, Polyphemus imprisoned them. Dashing out the brains of two men a day, he ate the men whole.

WHERE IN THE WORLD?

Cyclopes lived in the regions of Thrace in northeast Greece, in Lycia in southwest Turkey, and on the island of Crete. They worked in Hephaestus' forge on Lemnos, and built the cities of Mycenae and Tiryns. Later tales place them on Mount Etna in Sicily.

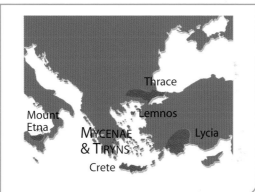

Thrace

Mount Etna

Lemnos

MYCENAE & TIRYNS

Lycia

Crete

DID YOU KNOW?

● The word "cyclops" comes from the Greek words kyklos ("circle") and ops ("eye"). The names of the cyclopes Brontes, Steropes and Arges meant "thunder," "lightning bolt," and "lightning flash."

● The cyclops myth may have its origins in an ancient guild of Greek metal-workers in Thrace, who had circles tattooed on their foreheads.

● Some people believe that the legend of the cyclopes arose when the Ancient Greeks first encountered elephants.

KRAKEN

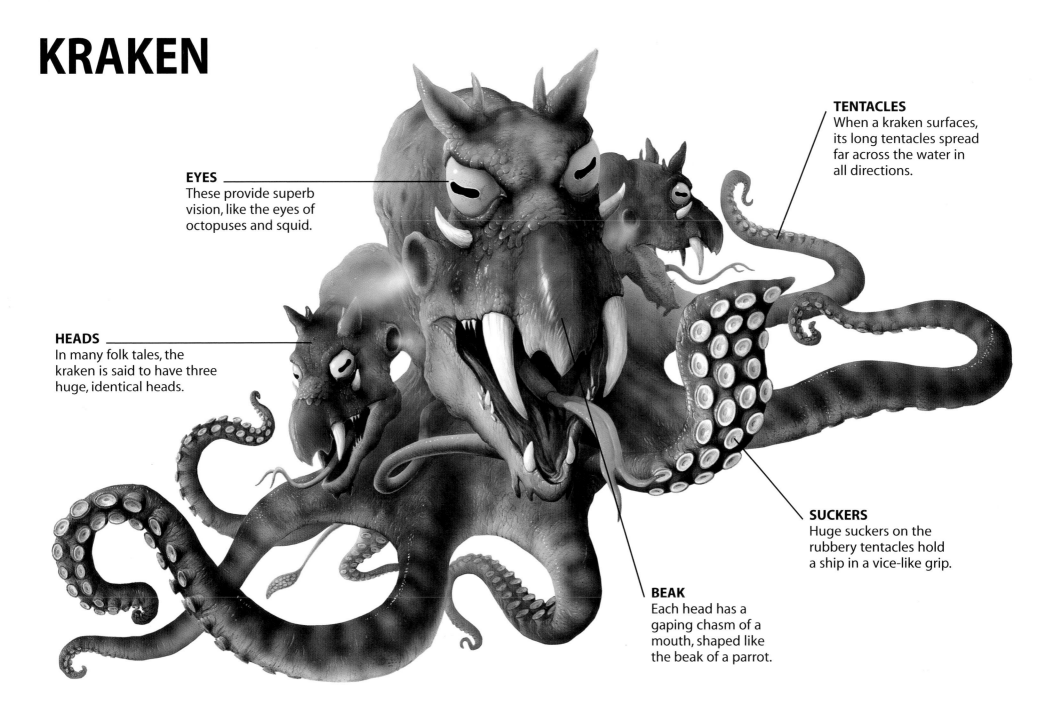

EYES
These provide superb vision, like the eyes of octopuses and squid.

HEADS
In many folk tales, the kraken is said to have three huge, identical heads.

TENTACLES
When a kraken surfaces, its long tentacles spread far across the water in all directions.

SUCKERS
Huge suckers on the rubbery tentacles hold a ship in a vice-like grip.

BEAK
Each head has a gaping chasm of a mouth, shaped like the beak of a parrot.

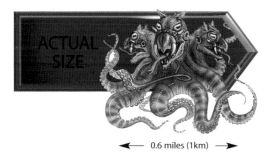

ACTUAL SIZE

← 0.6 miles (1km) →

Since medieval times, sailors and fishermen from western Europe— especially Scandinavia—have told of a vast, tentacled sea monster that lives in the ocean depths. The kraken is a mountain of a creature, dwarfing the largest of whales. In one book on the natural history of Norway, published in 1754, the Bishop of Bergen even claimed that the monster's body was almost 1.5 miles (2.5km) in circumference.

In the seas off northern Europe, a travel-weary captain sights land at last. His charts make no reference to the strangely rounded islands, but he trusts his eyes and steers his ship toward them. But as he draws closer, the captain realizes his mistake with horror. The "islands" erupt from the sea to reveal a huge kraken. The waking monster seizes the ship in a mighty tentacle and plunges it beneath the boiling waves. Grasping one of the crew with another, it lifts him, screaming, into a gaping beak.

WHERE IN THE WORLD?

Most of the legends tell us the kraken lived around the coasts of Scandinavia, especially in the deep waters off Norway. But similar tales also come from other coastal areas of Europe.

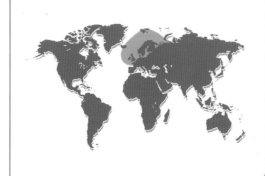

DID YOU KNOW?

● In some tales, the kraken has 1000 tentacles and 10 mouths.

● There are reports of accidental kraken strandings. In 1680, a young kraken supposedly died after it was caught on the reefs off Alstadhang in Norway. And in 1775, another was found on the Isle of Bute in Scotland.

● The English 19th-century poet Alfred, Lord Tennyson wrote a poem, "The Kraken," inspired by the myths.

GORGON

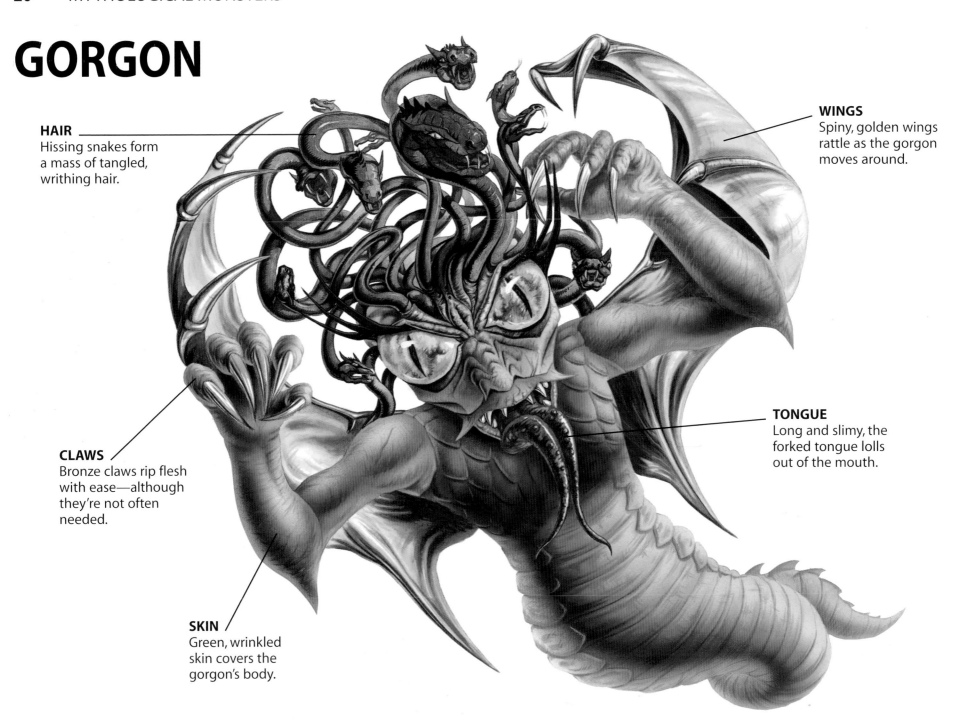

HAIR
Hissing snakes form a mass of tangled, writhing hair.

WINGS
Spiny, golden wings rattle as the gorgon moves around.

CLAWS
Bronze claws rip flesh with ease—although they're not often needed.

TONGUE
Long and slimy, the forked tongue lolls out of the mouth.

SKIN
Green, wrinkled skin covers the gorgon's body.

ACTUAL SIZE

Medusa is the only mortal gorgon. Her name means "the cunning one". In some versions of the myth, she is the only one of the three who can turn people to stone, but other versions say that all the gorgon sisters have this power.

Stheno and Euryale are Medusa's sisters, destined to share her awful fate. Both these gorgons are immortal, and in some versions of the myth, are slightly less hideous than their sister. The name Stheno means "the mighty one", and Euryale "the wide-roaming one".

Crumbling stone statues litter the gorgons' dreary lair, the petrified remains of onlookers who fell victim to the sisters' terrible powers. Humans aren't the only ones susceptible—even animals are turned to stone by the gruesome spectacle.

A gorgon is such a hideous spectacle, that one glance is enough to turn onlookers to stone. The gorgons were not always vile monsters. Once they were beautiful sisters, until Medusa offended the goddess Athena by seducing the sea god, Poseidon, in one of her temples. Athena was furious, and turned the sisters into hideous creatures. The hero Perseus killed the gorgon Medusa with help from the gods and from a highly polished shield. The shield acted like a mirror, which meant he did not have to look directly into Medusa's face. Perseus then used Medusa's severed head to turn his own enemies into statues.

WHERE IN THE WORLD?

The ancient Greeks believed the gorgons lived in the mythical land of the Hyperboreans, beyond the north wind on the shores of the ocean that encircled the Earth. The sources place this land as being the coast of Russia, Scandinavia or northeastern Europe.

DID YOU KNOW?

● According to legend when Perseus cut off Medusa's head, the winged horse Pegasus and a fully armed warrior called Chrysaor sprang from her body.

● As Perseus flew back to Greece, drops of Medusa's blood fell into the sea, instantly turning into coral known as gorgonia. More drops fell on the desert, where they became snakes.

● Athene gave two vials of gorgon blood to Asclepius, the founder of Greek medicine. She filled one from the veins on the left of Medusa's body, and the other from the veins on the right. Blood from the left side could raise the dead, while that from the right destroyed life.

MINOTAUR

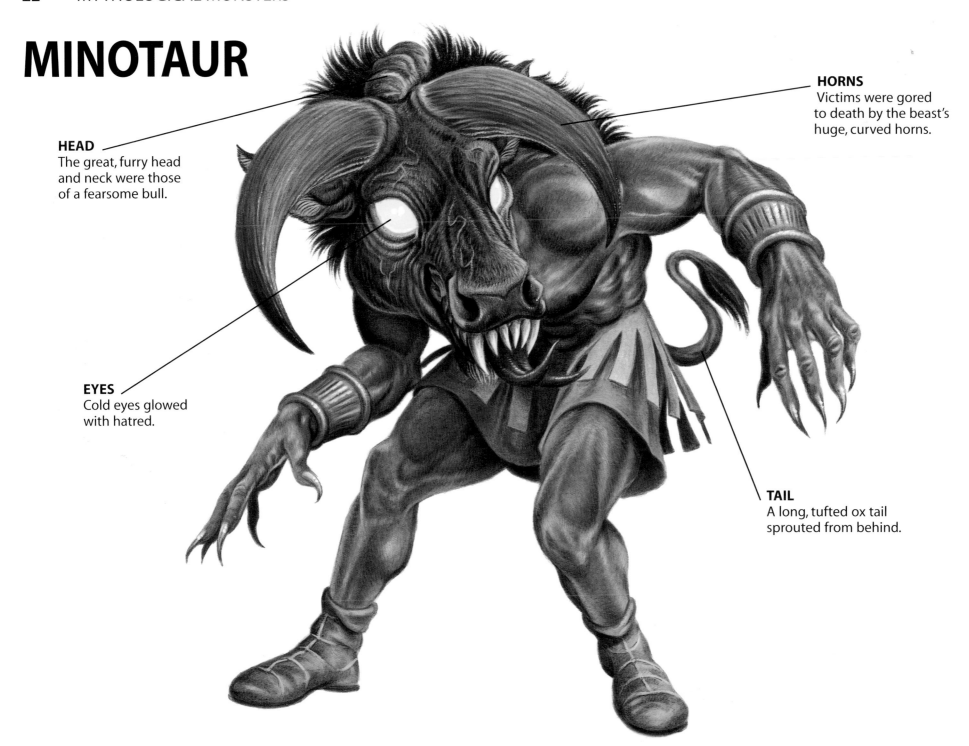

HEAD
The great, furry head and neck were those of a fearsome bull.

EYES
Cold eyes glowed with hatred.

HORNS
Victims were gored to death by the beast's huge, curved horns.

TAIL
A long, tufted ox tail sprouted from behind.

ACTUAL SIZE

The Minotaur was born after King Minos angered the sea-god Poseidon. Poseidon had sent a snow-white bull for Minos to sacrifice, but Minos couldn't bring himself to kill the bull. Poseidon was furious, and punished Minos by making his wife, Queen Pasiphae, fall in love with the animal. Pasiphae produced a child with a grotesque bull's head and a taste for human flesh. Minos ordered the master craftsman Daedalus to make a vast underground maze to house the monster. The Minotaur was put inside, where it remained lost in the darkness. Every so often, human victims were forced into the maze as sacrifices. The Minotaur was finally vanquished by Theseus, one of the great Greek heroes.

WHERE IN THE WORLD?

The mythical Minotaur was said to have lived at Knossos, on the island of Crete in the eastern Mediterranean. Theseus, who slew the beast, came from the city of Athens on the Greek mainland.

1 Theseus and his companions were sent from Athens as a sacrifice. Forced into the Labyrinth, they faced a maze of dark passages. Quickly, Theseus revealed his plan to the terrified Athenians, and told them to stay near the entrance while he went in search of the Minotaur, armed with a sword and a ball of thread.

2 Tying the end of the thread firmly to a doorpost, Theseus cautiously picked his way through the tunnels of the maze, unraveling the ball as he went. He knew that, after killing the beast, he would be able to retrace his steps and escape the maze by following the thread.

3 Suddenly, the terrible beast was upon him, snorting and charging with horns lowered. A desperate fight ensued, until, summoning all his strength and courage, Theseus plunged the sword through the Minotaur's neck, severing its head from its body.

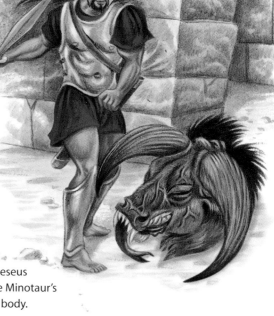

DID YOU KNOW?

● The story of Theseus slaying the Minotaur could be a symbolic version of real historical events, representing the Greek overthrow of Minoan power in 1450 BC.

● Artifacts from ancient Crete show athletes performing the death-defying bull-leaping ceremony. Each athlete would face a wild, charging bull, grasp its spiked horns, and vault or somersault over the animal's back.

● The Nemean lion was another Greek monster: a giant beast invulnerable to wounds.

ONI

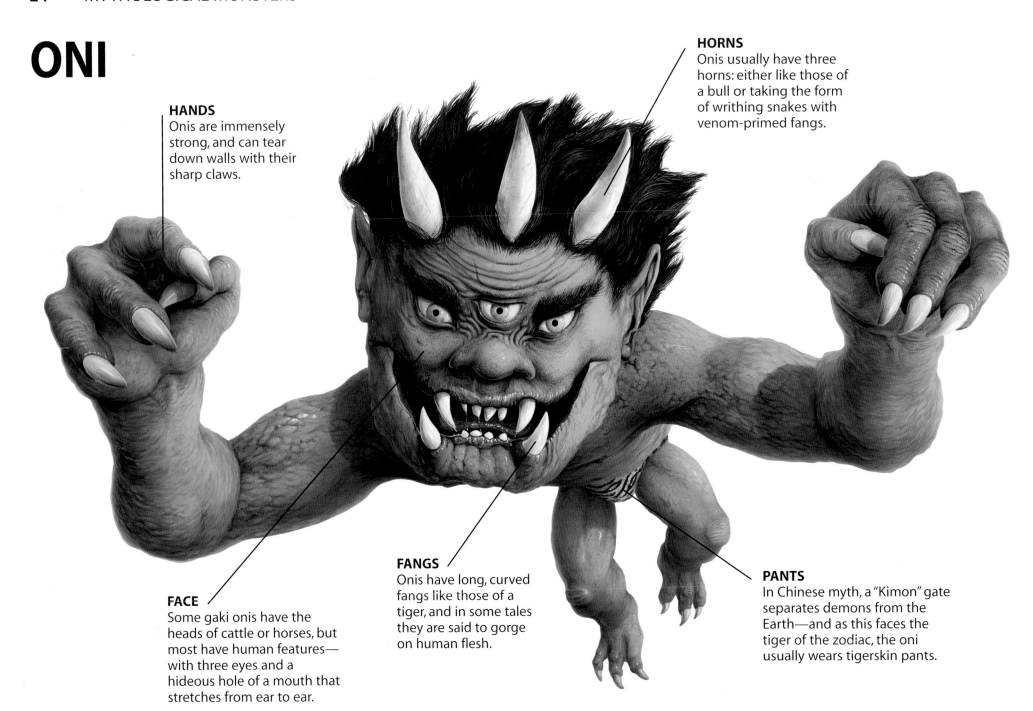

HANDS
Onis are immensely strong, and can tear down walls with their sharp claws.

HORNS
Onis usually have three horns: either like those of a bull or taking the form of writhing snakes with venom-primed fangs.

FACE
Some gaki onis have the heads of cattle or horses, but most have human features—with three eyes and a hideous hole of a mouth that stretches from ear to ear.

FANGS
Onis have long, curved fangs like those of a tiger, and in some tales they are said to gorge on human flesh.

PANTS
In Chinese myth, a "Kimon" gate separates demons from the Earth—and as this faces the tiger of the zodiac, the oni usually wears tigerskin pants.

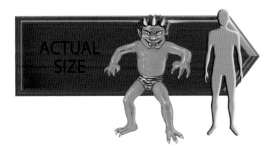

ACTUAL SIZE

Whistling gaily as it works, this ghastly creature delights in tormenting the people of Japan, avoiding detection by flitting invisibly through the air or taking human form. Once a Shinto god, it became an evil spirit after Buddhism spread into Japan from China in the 6th century CE. In earthly guise it causes disasters, famine and disease, while its demonic form steals sinners' souls. Many Onis have green or red skin. They suffer continual hunger and often have enormous bellies. Hunting down sinners, they take them in a fiery chariot to hell.

The inhabitants of this small Japanese village are blissfully unaware that the extremely dangerous Oni is hovering above, waiting to cast its evil spell on them. As it swirls above the village considering what damage it can cause, the residents are getting on with their everyday lives, unaware that their lives are about to be completely transformed. What devastation the Oni will bring, nobody knows. Its sheer strength and power could cast a spell causing a terrifying earthquake, a deadly disease or even a terrible famine.

WHERE IN THE WORLD?

Onis living in the mortal world are found almost exclusively in Japan, although they are thought to have originated in China. Other onis known as gaki inhabit the spirit world or Jigoku (hell) underground.

DID YOU KNOW?

● A woman may turn into an oni under the stress of jealousy or grief, while other onis may be the souls of people who died of plague or famine.

● The Buddhist sage Nichiren regarded the onis as a punishment for the sins of the Japanese, so he founded a school to reform people.

● Although female onis take the form of beautiful women, they are prone to violent outbursts of rage.

THUNDERBIRD

BACK
The thunderbird can carry an entire lake of water on its mighty back, releasing the water in torrential downpours.

EYES
Each time the thunderbird opens its eyes, bolts of lightning flash from the sky.

WINGS
Powerful wings with feathers as long as canoe paddles send claps of thunder echoing through the air.

HEADS
A second head sprouts from the thunderbird's chest, and both are equipped with viciously hooked beaks.

FEET
Huge, curved talons tip each toe, like those of a giant eagle or vulture.

The Nootka people of Vancouver Island, off British Columbia, called the thunderbird Tootooch. To them, it was the sole survivor of four giant birds that preyed on whales (left, a sperm whale). By turning into a whale, the god Quawteaht tricked the birds into attacking him. He lured three to their death as he dived deep, but the survivor flew to the heavens. The story probably reflects the fact that storms often come from just one point on the compass. In the tales of the Quillayute people of the Olympic Peninsula in Washington State, the thunderbird and killer whale are deadly enemies. They once fought a fierce battle, shaking the mountains and uprooting trees as they struggled, creating vast treeless plains. Every time the thunderbird seized the whale in its talons, the whale managed to escape, finally retreating into the deep ocean.

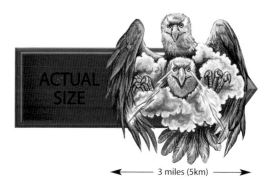

ACTUAL SIZE

← 3 miles (5km) →

This gigantic two-headed bird-of-prey is known by Native American tribes to bring thunder and lightning to the skies. Lightning bolts shoot from its eyes, storm clouds are carried on its wings, and an entire lake of water on its back makes torrential downpours. Yet in Native American mythology, the thunderbird means different things to different tribes. Some tribes believe that the thunderbird is even the great creator spirit that made the heavens and the earth. Native tribes in Africa and Australia also have similar traditions to the thunderbird, no doubt inspired by the sight of eagles or vultures circling high up in the skies.

WHERE IN THE WORLD?

Thunderbirds are part of the belief systems that were held by many different groups of Native Americans, from the Inuit peoples in the Arctic, to the Aztecs in Mexico. These gigantic birds are thought to live either in the sky or in remote mountain caves.

DID YOU KNOW?

● Many American tribes claim to have seen the thunderbird, and in South Dakota they believe it has left huge footprints. The prints are 25 miles (40km) apart in an area known as Thunder Tracks, near the source of St. Peter's River.

● Some stories say that the thunderbird lives in a mountain cave, burying its food in a dark hole in the ice. If hunters come too close, it rolls huge lumps of ice down the mountainside to scare them away.

GRIFFIN

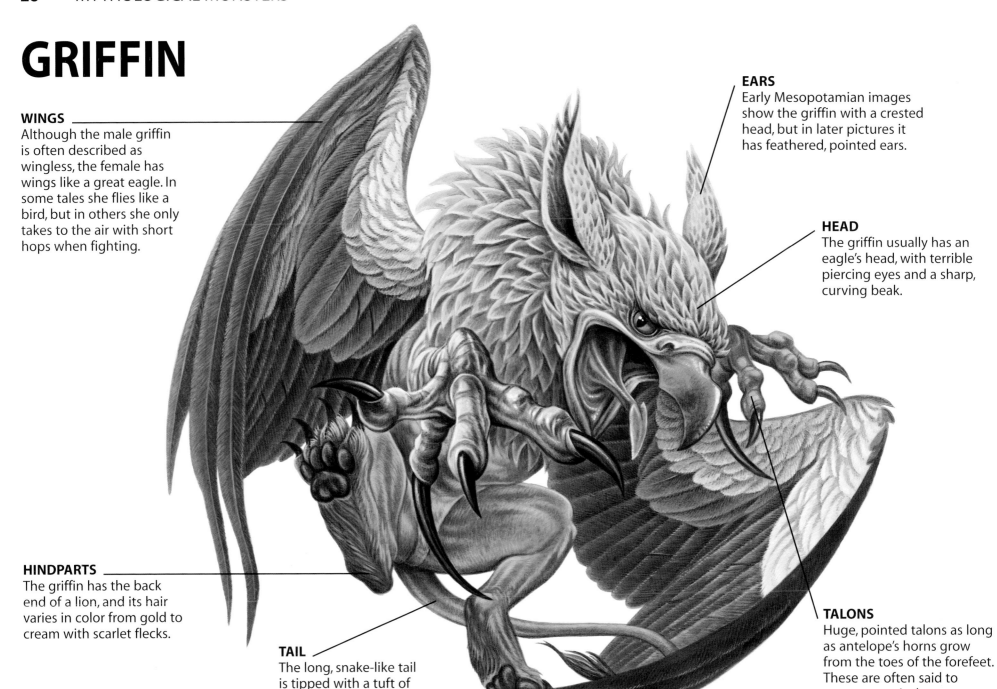

WINGS
Although the male griffin is often described as wingless, the female has wings like a great eagle. In some tales she flies like a bird, but in others she only takes to the air with short hops when fighting.

EARS
Early Mesopotamian images show the griffin with a crested head, but in later pictures it has feathered, pointed ears.

HEAD
The griffin usually has an eagle's head, with terrible piercing eyes and a sharp, curving beak.

HINDPARTS
The griffin has the back end of a lion, and its hair varies in color from gold to cream with scarlet flecks.

TAIL
The long, snake-like tail is tipped with a tuft of hair like that of a lion.

TALONS
Huge, pointed talons as long as antelope's horns grow from the toes of the forefeet. These are often said to possess magical powers.

ACTUAL SIZE

This ferocious mythological beast has the head, wings and forelegs of an eagle, and the hindquarters of a lion. Given to attacking other animals at will, it's also said to tear up humans on sight with its slashing claws and tearing beak. The griffin is a colossally powerful predator that can carry off a yoke of oxen in its claws—in some medieval accounts, it is stronger than eight lions and 100 eagles. It also hoards gold and emeralds, fiercely attacking anyone who tries to steal from its nest.

Many griffins were said to live in the ancient land of Scythia, north of the Black Sea—an area rich in gold and jewels. Digging up these treasures with their claws, they used them to line their nests. The Arimaspians wanted these riches, too and often rode on horseback into battle with the griffins. As a result, griffins attacked horses whenever they could. Gripping with their scythe-like claws, they hacked in with the hooked bill, leaving terrible, bloody wounds.

WHERE IN THE WORLD?

Griffins were thought to live in various parts of the Near and Middle East, from Egypt, Greece and Turkey through to Syria, Iraq, Iran and Armenia. They were also strongly associated with India and southern parts of the former Soviet Union.

DID YOU KNOW?

● Artifacts from Ancient Greece sometimes show the griffin with a mane of tightly coiled curls.

● One Norse legend tells of Prince Hagen, who was carried away to a griffin's nest. Fortunately he found a suit of armor and managed to kill the young griffins as they attacked.

● The female griffin lays eggs like those of an eagle. Her young are far more gentle than an adret.

DRACULA

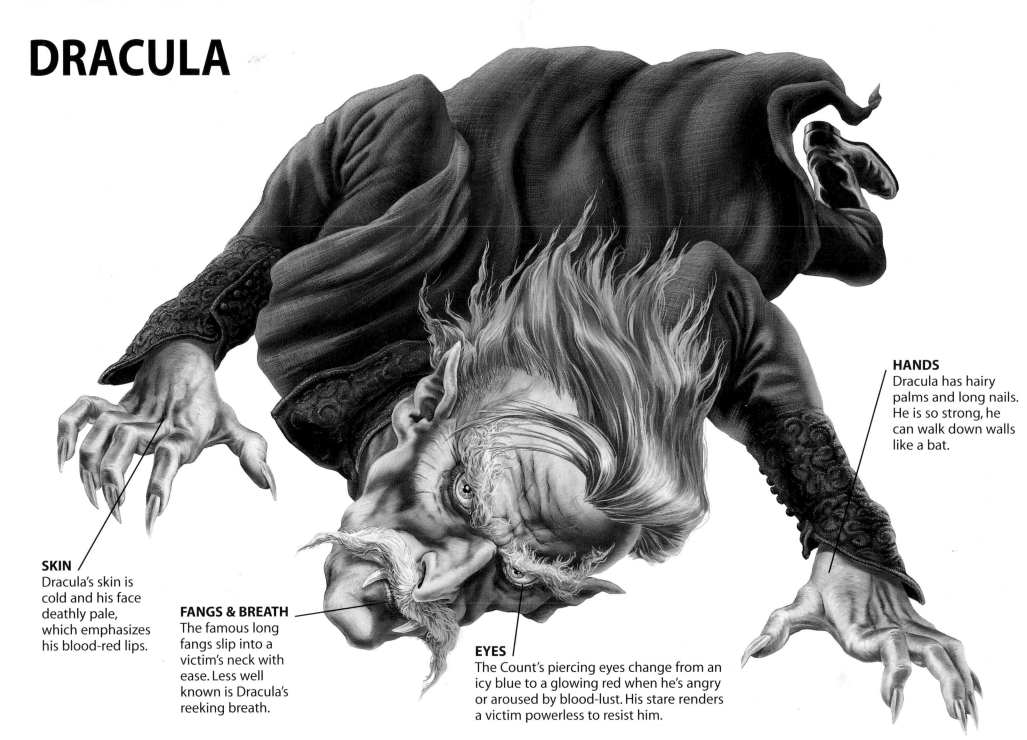

HANDS
Dracula has hairy palms and long nails. He is so strong, he can walk down walls like a bat.

SKIN
Dracula's skin is cold and his face deathly pale, which emphasizes his blood-red lips.

FANGS & BREATH
The famous long fangs slip into a victim's neck with ease. Less well known is Dracula's reeking breath.

EYES
The Count's piercing eyes change from an icy blue to a glowing red when he's angry or aroused by blood-lust. His stare renders a victim powerless to resist him.

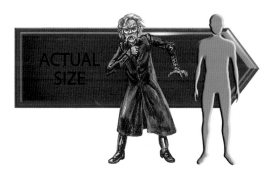

ACTUAL SIZE

In his famous book *Dracula* (1897), Bram Stoker conjured up a true nightmare: a creature of the dark who feasts on human blood, infecting his victims with vampirism. Dracula was a centuries-old vampire, an "undead" being who drank people's blood to stay immortal—turning them into vampires, too. He lived in a remote castle high in the mountains of Transylvania in Romania, and had the power to change into a bat, a dog or a cloud of mist to carry out his foul deeds.

Bram Stoker's dark tale ends with a brave team of vampire-hunters, including one Jonathan Harker and his friend Quincey Morris, chasing the Count from England back to Transylvania. Within sight of Dracula's castle, they finally catch up with the Count in his horse-drawn box just as night is falling. Harker and Morris burst past the vampire's helpers, hurl the the box from the cart and rip it open. The waking Count's eyes burn red with hate and triumph, but even as the sun sets and his powers return, Harker chops off his head and Morris plunges a knife deep into his heart. Within seconds, Dracula crumbles into dust. His evil rule is ended at last.

WHERE IN THE WORLD?

Dracula's ancestral home is a castle in the mountains of Transylvania in Romania. In the story, he sails to Whitby in northern England, moves on to London, then is chased back to his castle, where his reign of terror finally ends.

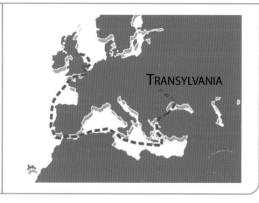

TRANSYLVANIA

DID YOU KNOW?

● Bram Stoker was inspired to write *Dracula* by a disturbing dream in which a Count stops a beautiful young woman kissing his throat, saying "This man belongs to me".

● Stoker chose the name Dracula after reading about Vlad Dracula, a cruel ruler in Romania in the 15th century. "Dracula" means "devil" in a Romanian language.

● Vlad Dracula is also called Vlad the Impaler, as he impaled enemies on wooden stakes.

FRANKENSTEIN'S MONSTER

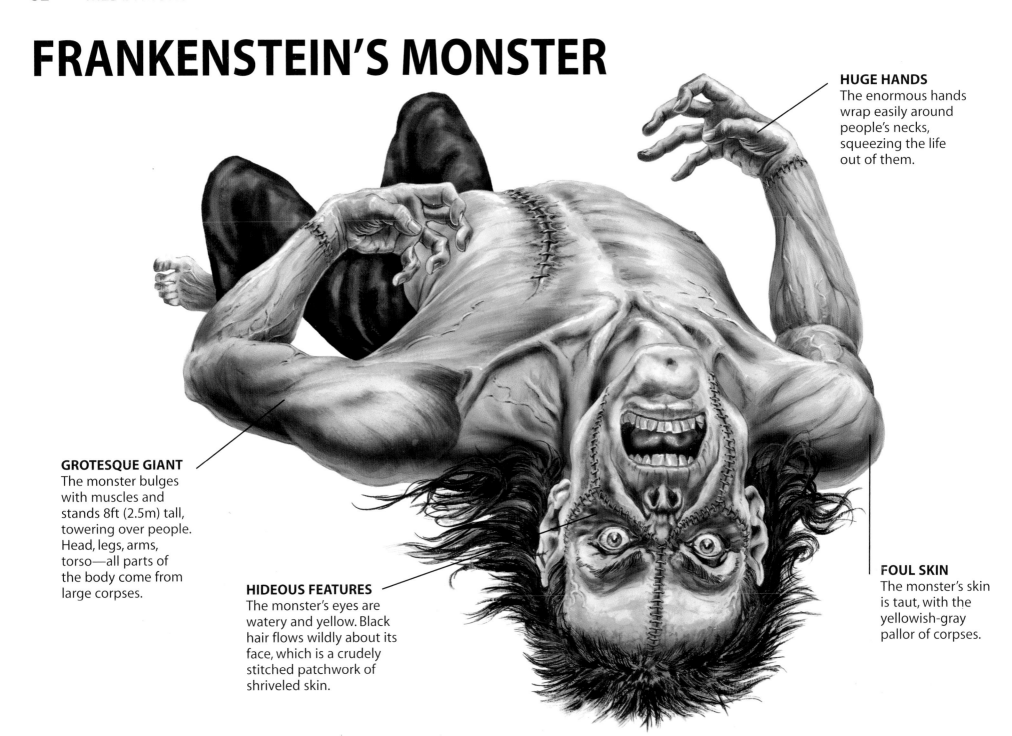

HUGE HANDS
The enormous hands wrap easily around people's necks, squeezing the life out of them.

GROTESQUE GIANT
The monster bulges with muscles and stands 8ft (2.5m) tall, towering over people. Head, legs, arms, torso—all parts of the body come from large corpses.

HIDEOUS FEATURES
The monster's eyes are watery and yellow. Black hair flows wildly about its face, which is a crudely stitched patchwork of shriveled skin.

FOUL SKIN
The monster's skin is taut, with the yellowish-gray pallor of corpses.

ACTUAL SIZE

Frankenstein's evil monster is one of mankind's worst nightmares: a beast created by a mad scientist that wreaks murderous havoc on all around it. He is a giant creature sewn together from pieces of stolen bodies, brought mysteriously to life and endowed with superhuman strength. He then seeks revenge on the world when rejected by his creator, Victor Frankenstein. The monster was dreamed up one stormy night in 1816 by a young English woman, Mary Godwin (who became Mary Shelley).

WHERE IN THE WORLD?

Frankenstein created his monster in the town of Ingolstadt in southern Germany. The monster then follows its creator to the Alps, Britain and Geneva. Frankenstein then pursues it to the Mediterranean, the Black Sea and finally the Arctic Ocean.

DID YOU KNOW?

● In 1831, Mary Shelley explained how the story of Frankenstein came about. In the summer of 1816 she was with Percy Shelley, the poet Lord Byron, Byron's mistress Clare Clairemont and his doctor, John Polidori, in Switzerland. The weather was bad one night and they couldn't go out, so they decided that each would write a horror story: the result was Mary's novel *Frankenstein*.

● *Frankenstein* was published in 1818—anonymously. Critics assumed that the author was a man and were outraged when they discovered that a woman had written the book.

● In telling her story, Mary Shelley was influenced by the discovery of galvanism. In 1791, Luigi Galvani, an Italian scientist, found that electricity made the legs of a dead frog twitch. Then, in 1803, his nephew Luigi Aldini passed electricity through the corpse of a murderer hanged only

GODZILLA

JAWS
The jaws contain ranks of metal-strong teeth, but also give out a radioactive beam that is lethal to humans and destructive to buildings.

ARMS
These are used for punching and gripping. Godzilla often grabs hold of enemies and hurls them into the distance.

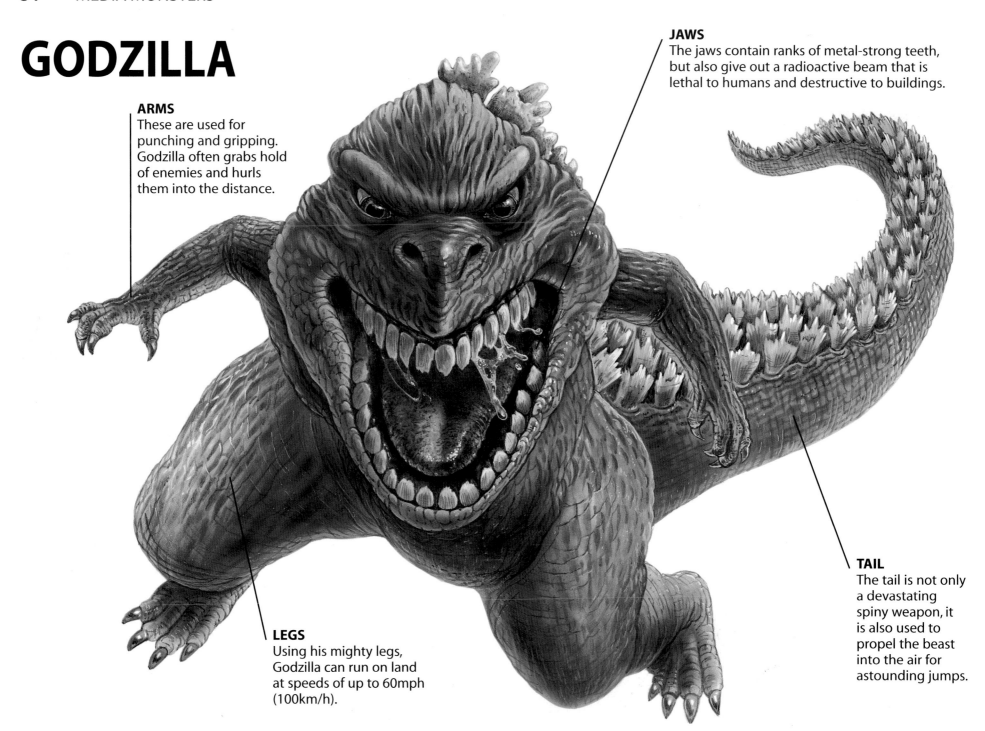

TAIL
The tail is not only a devastating spiny weapon, it is also used to propel the beast into the air for astounding jumps.

LEGS
Using his mighty legs, Godzilla can run on land at speeds of up to 60mph (100km/h).

ACTUAL SIZE

300ft (91m)

Godzilla was a remnant of the prehistoric age, a species of dinosaur known as the Godzillosaurus. Injured and awakened by US shelling during the Pacific War, the great beast mutated following later atomic bomb tests in the region, and grew to a height of over 300ft (91m). Then, turning upon the world that awoke him from prehistoric slumber, Godzilla unleashes a truly awesome destructive power. He is almost indestructible, with modern bullets and bombs bouncing off his armor-like hide. He also has weapons of his own, including (depending on the storyline) a lethal atomic energy beam that he fires from his vast and gaping jaws.

While swimming out at sea—where he moves underwater with the speed of a military submarine—Godzilla spots the sparkling lights of Tokyo on the horizon. He moves toward them, and the Tokyo citizens see his enormous bulk rise out of the harbor waters. Godzilla plunges into the heart of the city, smashing down entire skyscrapers with his tail and crushing cars, trucks and people under his massive feet. Having obliterated much of Tokyo's city center, Godzilla then slips back into the

WHERE IN THE WORLD?

Godzilla has traveled the world in print and film, but his origins lie on the island of Lagos, near the Marshall Islands in the southern Pacific Ocean. It is a tropical region devastated during World War II.

Marshall Islands ●

DID YOU KNOW?

● Godzilla first appeared on movie screens in 1954, the film coming from the Japanese Toho Co. Ltd. His original name was "Gojira", but this changed to Godzilla to meet the needs of American audiences.

● Throughout his monstrous career in film and comicbooks, Godzilla has battled with numerous monster and alien enemies. His foes include King Kong, Mothra and Titanosaurus.

● "Gojira" combines the Japanese names for gorilla and whale.

KING KONG

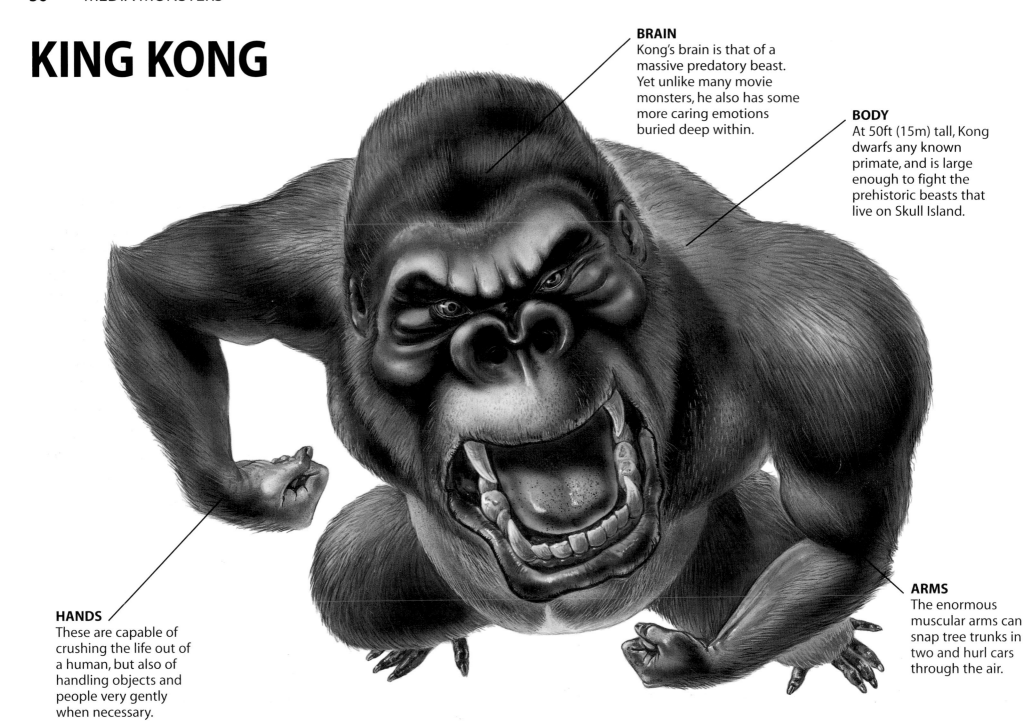

BRAIN
Kong's brain is that of a massive predatory beast. Yet unlike many movie monsters, he also has some more caring emotions buried deep within.

BODY
At 50ft (15m) tall, Kong dwarfs any known primate, and is large enough to fight the prehistoric beasts that live on Skull Island.

ARMS
The enormous muscular arms can snap tree trunks in two and hurl cars through the air.

HANDS
These are capable of crushing the life out of a human, but also of handling objects and people very gently when necessary.

Having escaped from his chains of imprisonment on Broadway, the mighty Kong smashes through New York in anger, while also searching for his human love, Ann Darrow. He plucks Ann from a local hotel, and gently carries her across town in one hand—the other hand crushes trains, cars and buildings with horrifying ease. Finally, Kong ascends the Empire State Building, and places Ann on a ledge to fight off an attack by four US Navy biplanes. He manages to snatch one of the aircraft from the air, smashing it like matchwood. However, his end is near. Riddled by machine-gun bullets, he eventually dies and his enormous body plunges down into the streets below.

50ft (15m)

King Kong is the ultimate natural powerhouse, and a true movie legend. The first film bearing his name hit the screens in 1933, and he stunned audiences with his crunching aggression and also his unexpected tenderness. In the story, an American film crew encounter Kong on a mysterious island in the Pacific, known as Skull Island. They eventually capture the great beast, shipping it back to New York to display in Broadway shows. It escapes, and crashes through the New York jungle, finally ending it days atop the Empire State Building. Yet along the way, it also falls in love with a human, Ann Darrow.

WHERE IN THE WORLD?

Kong was captured on the remote "Skull Island" in the Pacific, a mysterious place inhabited by prehistoric beasts and violent tribespeople. From there he was transported by ship back to New York, where he is finally killed.

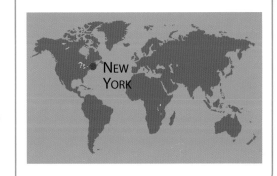

NEW YORK

DID YOU KNOW?

● King Kong has appeared in numerous movies since his first appearance in 1933. These include the Japanese film *King Kong vs. Godzilla* in 1966 and the 2005 epic *King Kong*, directed by Peter Jackson who also directed the *Lord of the Rings* trilogy of films.

● The original *King Kong* movie amazed the audiences of the 1930s with the stunning special effects, which convincingly mixed real people with animated models.

● Kong has lost none of his popularity—the 2005 *King Kong* took over $50 million in its first weekend.

WEREWOLF

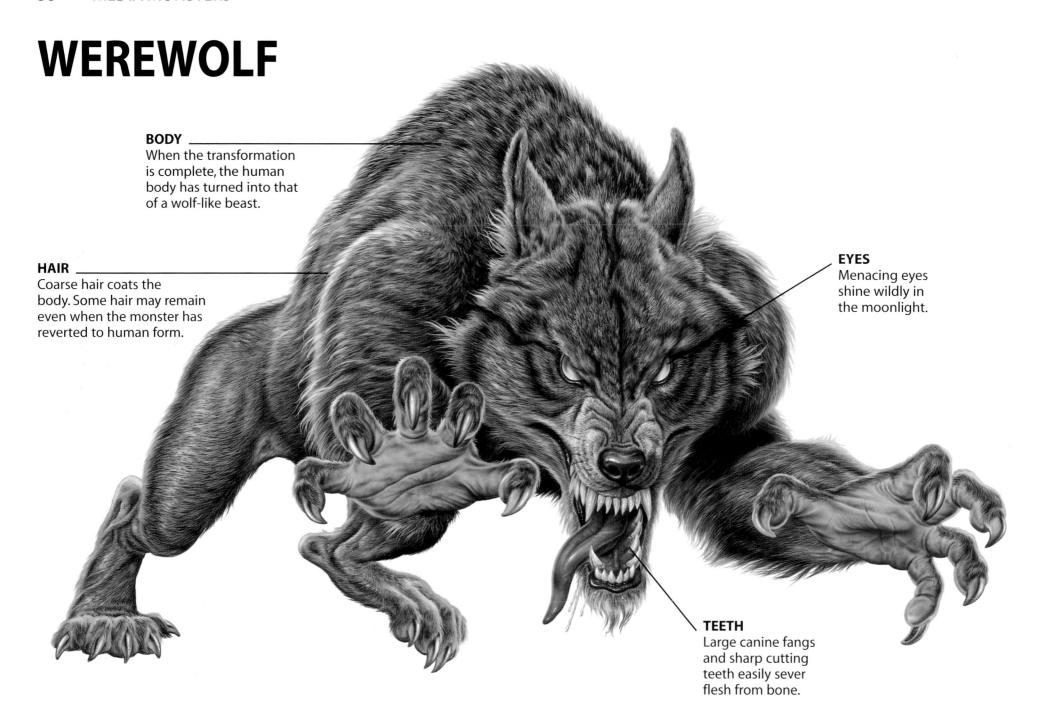

BODY
When the transformation is complete, the human body has turned into that of a wolf-like beast.

HAIR
Coarse hair coats the body. Some hair may remain even when the monster has reverted to human form.

EYES
Menacing eyes shine wildly in the moonlight.

TEETH
Large canine fangs and sharp cutting teeth easily sever flesh from bone.

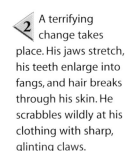

1 As the full moon rises into the sky and moonbeams strike his body, a man is racked with sudden pain: the curse has been activated.

2 A terrifying change takes place. His jaws stretch, his teeth enlarge into fangs, and hair breaks through his skin. He scrabbles wildly at his clothing with sharp, glinting claws.

3 By dawn, the werewolf has turned back into a man and lies exhausted in the cemetery, blissfully unaware of his earlier crimes.

An innocent-looking human by day, a werewolf changes by night into a terrifying wolfish beast. It attacks victims with vicious claws and fangs, tearing the flesh from their bones, or digs up corpses from cemeteries to satisfy its ravenous hunger for human flesh. The belief in werewolves probably grew from the fear of wolves, whose ghostly howls could be heard through the night-time forests. Belief in werewolves was particularly strong in medieval Europe, and hundreds of innocent people were horribly executed by fearful mobs. Some really believed they were werewolves and confessed to their "crimes". In fact, they were suffering from a madness known as lycanthropy.

WHERE IN THE WORLD?

Werewolf legends arose in many parts of Europe, Asia and North America inhabited by true wolves. The forests of France inspired the most stories: 30,000 cases were reported between 1520 and 1630.

DID YOU KNOW?

● In medieval Europe, people were regularly tried for being werewolves. One of the last convictions took place in 1720 in Salzburg, Austria.

● Many people believed that werewolves disguised themselves by hiding their hair inside their bodies. Suspects were often torn apart as prosecutors searched for evidence.

● Folk stories from around the world tell of people who change into tigers, leopards, hyenas and bears. Some even describe werepigs, which attack and bite passers-by.

● In European folklore, werewolves sometimes turn into vampires as they die, continuing their reign of terror.

REPTOID ALIEN

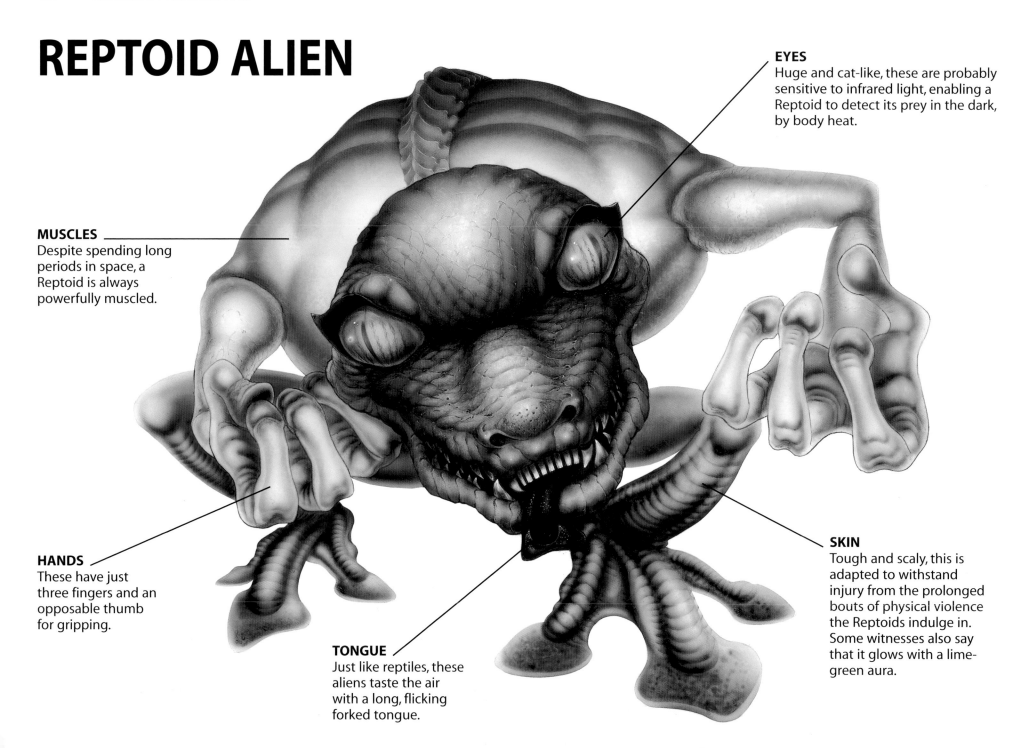

EYES
Huge and cat-like, these are probably sensitive to infrared light, enabling a Reptoid to detect its prey in the dark, by body heat.

MUSCLES
Despite spending long periods in space, a Reptoid is always powerfully muscled.

HANDS
These have just three fingers and an opposable thumb for gripping.

TONGUE
Just like reptiles, these aliens taste the air with a long, flicking forked tongue.

SKIN
Tough and scaly, this is adapted to withstand injury from the prolonged bouts of physical violence the Reptoids indulge in. Some witnesses also say that it glows with a lime-green aura.

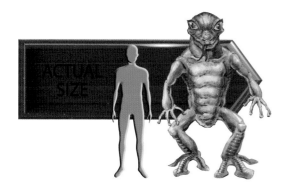

ACTUAL SIZE

These scaly monsters seem to enjoy kidnapping both animals and human beings—so keep on eye on the skies. Some people claim they are aliens, while others think they are descendants of the dinosaurs. Whatever the case, they have supposedly left a trail of horribly mutilated animals across the United States. As well as being brutal and violent, the Reptoid alien is also highly intelligent. It is feared by some that one day they may take control of our planet, putting humans into the chains of slavery.

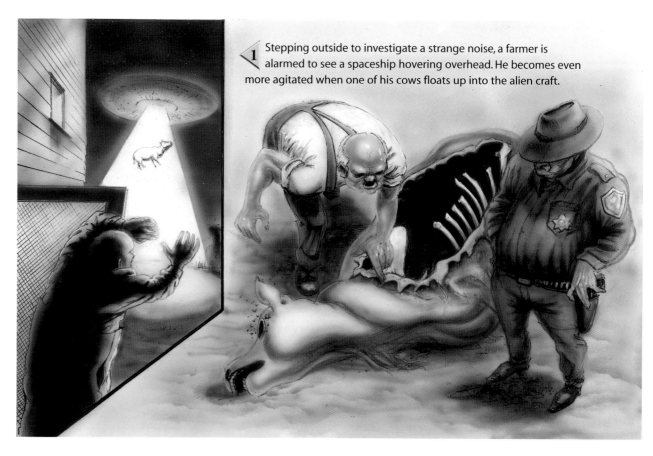

1 Stepping outside to investigate a strange noise, a farmer is alarmed to see a spaceship hovering overhead. He becomes even more agitated when one of his cows floats up into the alien craft.

WHERE IN THE WORLD?

Reports of Reptoid aliens come from around the world, but these entities are most active in remote areas of the USA. Why the Reptoids favor these regions is unknown, but it seems they wish to operate without interference from the authorities.

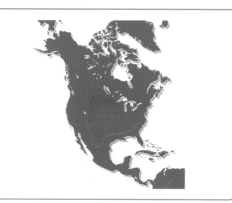

2 Next day, he finds one of his cows drained of blood and with its eyes, tongue and innards surgically removed. But despite the evidence, the sheriff refuses to believe his story.

DID YOU KNOW?

● Some experts speculate that the Reptoids consider a cow's blood and organs a delicacy; others think they use the cows as an organic resource.

● Abductees say that the Reptoids come from the Draco star system.

● Some UFOlogists claim that the Reptoids avoid arousing suspicion by transporting their invasion force safely between stars in a massive spaceship disguised as a planet.

JERSEY DEVIL

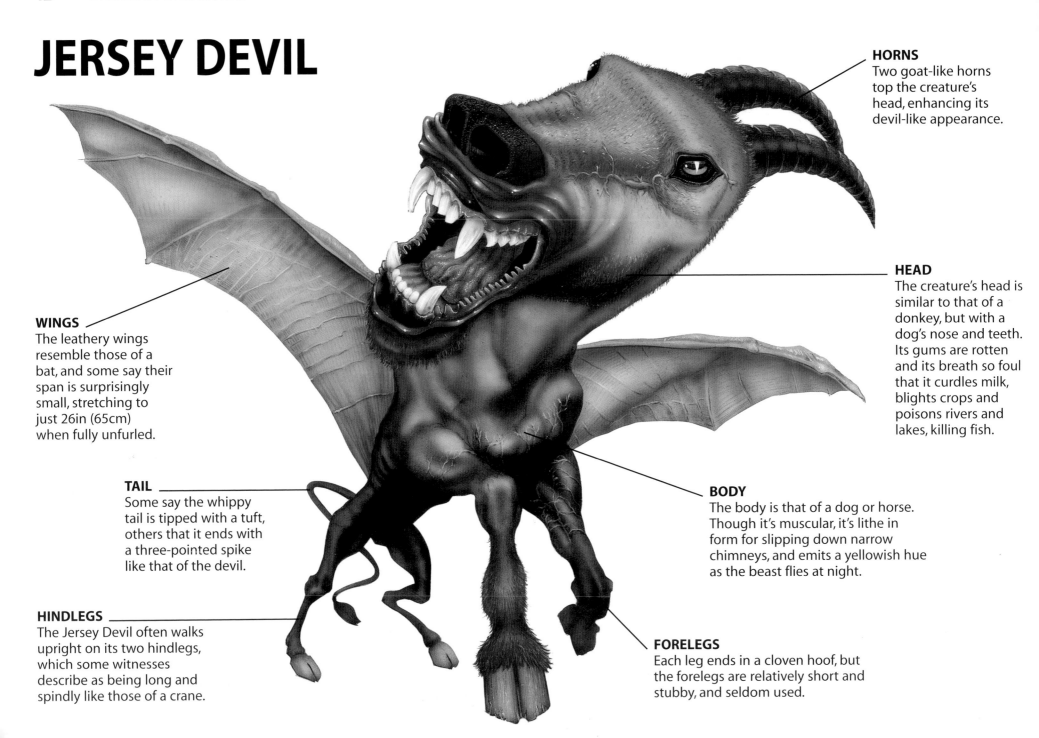

HORNS
Two goat-like horns top the creature's head, enhancing its devil-like appearance.

HEAD
The creature's head is similar to that of a donkey, but with a dog's nose and teeth. Its gums are rotten and its breath so foul that it curdles milk, blights crops and poisons rivers and lakes, killing fish.

WINGS
The leathery wings resemble those of a bat, and some say their span is surprisingly small, stretching to just 26in (65cm) when fully unfurled.

BODY
The body is that of a dog or horse. Though it's muscular, it's lithe in form for slipping down narrow chimneys, and emits a yellowish hue as the beast flies at night.

TAIL
Some say the whippy tail is tipped with a tuft, others that it ends with a three-pointed spike like that of the devil.

HINDLEGS
The Jersey Devil often walks upright on its two hindlegs, which some witnesses describe as being long and spindly like those of a crane.

FORELEGS
Each leg ends in a cloven hoof, but the forelegs are relatively short and stubby, and seldom used.

The bleak marshes of New Jersey in the USA have never welcomed people, and locals tell of strange sightings and chilling cries in the dark. According to many, something evil is out there. With bat-like wings and the head of a deformed horse, this inexplicable beast has been terrifying locals for more than 200 years. The devil emerges in the dead of night to haunt the countryside, killing wild and domestic animals and abducting small children. In January 1909, in a single week, more than 1000 people said they came face-to-face with the Jersey Devil, which appeared to householders, policemen and local officials. The accounts were all very similar, and local and national newspapers were forced to take the story seriously.

Driven mad by hunger, the Jersey Devil leaves its dismal swampy home and flies to a nearby town, a glowing shadow in the night sky. After cruising over the rooftops, it spots a suitable chimney and dives swiftly down the soot-laden stack. The devil is unscathed by the fierce fire burning in the grate and bursts through the flames, scattering logs into the kitchen beyond. Screaming in terror at the nightmare vision, a maid watches in horror as the devil makes for the larder. She can only pray that the child upstairs remains silent—for a single cry might tempt the ravenous beast to sample fresher food…

WHERE IN THE WORLD?

Many sightings of the Jersey Devil occur in the Pine Barrens of New Jersey: a lonely area of swamps and cedar forests covering 1698 sq miles (4400 sq km). But other reports come from all around the state, and occasionally from across the border.

DID YOU KNOW?

● In 1909, Philadelphia Zoo offered a $10,000 reward for the capture of the devil. This has prompted several hoaxes, including a painted kangaroo with a set of false wings. The reward remains to be claimed to this day.

● When the rotting corpse of a strange, devilish creature was found in the Pine Barrens in 1957, many people took this as evidence that the Jersey Devil was dead. But since then there have been several sightings.

LOCH NESS MONSTER

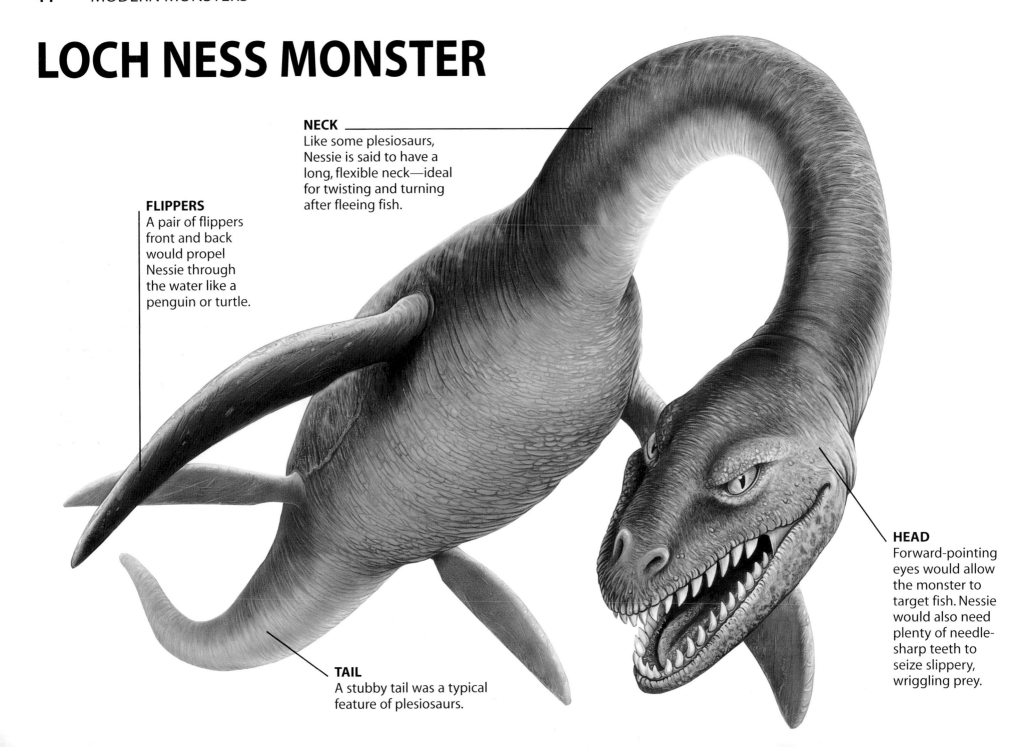

NECK
Like some plesiosaurs,
Nessie is said to have a
long, flexible neck—ideal
for twisting and turning
after fleeing fish.

FLIPPERS
A pair of flippers
front and back
would propel
Nessie through
the water like a
penguin or turtle.

TAIL
A stubby tail was a typical
feature of plesiosaurs.

HEAD
Forward-pointing
eyes would allow
the monster to
target fish. Nessie
would also need
plenty of needle-
sharp teeth to
seize slippery,
wriggling prey.

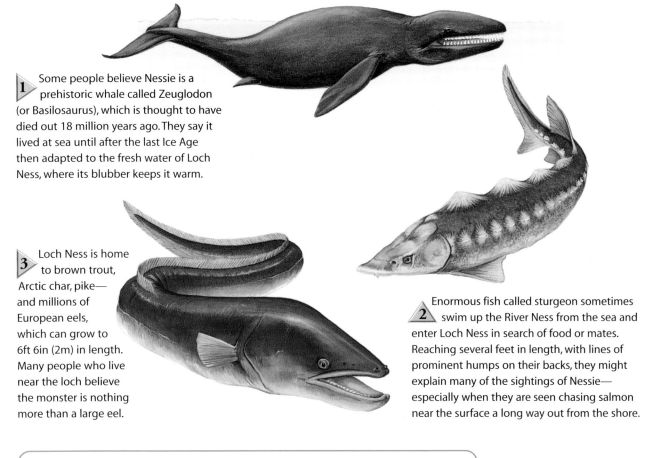

1 Some people believe Nessie is a prehistoric whale called Zeuglodon (or Basilosaurus), which is thought to have died out 18 million years ago. They say it lived at sea until after the last Ice Age then adapted to the fresh water of Loch Ness, where its blubber keeps it warm.

3 Loch Ness is home to brown trout, Arctic char, pike—and millions of European eels, which can grow to 6ft 6in (2m) in length. Many people who live near the loch believe the monster is nothing more than a large eel.

2 Enormous fish called sturgeon sometimes swim up the River Ness from the sea and enter Loch Ness in search of food or mates. Reaching several feet in length, with lines of prominent humps on their backs, they might explain many of the sightings of Nessie—especially when they are seen chasing salmon near the surface a long way out from the shore.

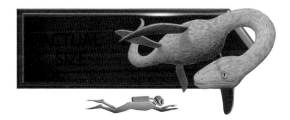

Legend has long had it that something strange lurks in the dark depths of Loch Ness—and since the 1930s, thousands of people have claimed to have seen a hump-backed, long-necked beast there. Some people claim that the "Loch Ness Monster" is actually a dinosaur whose species survives to this day in the cold Scottish waters. Other people say that the whole monster story is simply a myth invented by imaginative people. Whatever the reality, the fact remains that a number of people claim to have seen the monster. Even today the loch attracts tourists hoping to catch sight of "Nessie."

WHERE IN THE WORLD?

Loch Ness is part of a chain of lochs, rivers and canals in the Great Glen, a geological fault that runs right across the Scottish Highlands from the North Sea to the Atlantic Ocean. The River Ness links the loch to the North Sea.

DID YOU KNOW?

● There is not a single recorded sighting of Nessie before 1930.

● A handful of claimed sightings have been on land, including one of the first, on 22 July 1933. A Mr. and Mrs. Spicer reported that a monster crossed the road in front of their car as they drove along the loch.

● Scientists who believe the Loch Ness monster exists have given it a Latin name: Nessitera rhombopteryx.

BIGFOOT

ARMS
The arms are long in proportion to the body, hanging down to the knees or even below.

FACE
Bigfoot has a heavy brow ridge and wide, ape-like nostrils. Its eyes may shine green or yellow.

SIZE
Bigfoot measures more than 3ft 3in (1m) wide, and has a stooping posture and broad, sloping shoulders. Its weight is estimated at 400–440lb (181–200kg).

HAIR
One of Bigfoot's most distinctive features is a thick covering of hair. Usually, this coat is shaggy and brown, but some people have described rust-colored, black or even glossy hair.

This terrifying, ape-like creature is said to roam in remote mountain forests, but it has eluded researchers and baffled sceptics for more than 150 years. Standing well over 6ft 6in (2m) high, with arms down to its knees, Bigfoot can easily carry away dogs and livestock. More than 1600 instances of Bigfoot sightings or trails have been recorded in the United States and Canada since the early 19th century.

GIGANTOPITHECUS
This giant ape was the largest primate ever to live on Earth. Fossils of two species have been found in India and China, dating from between one and nine million years ago. Scientists think the ape lived in open country, but they don't know if it walked upright.

YETI
Although there have been few actual sightings of the Himalayan abominable snowman, or Yeti, many people have come across its distinctive tracks. Some who have seen the Yeti describe a creature with pale or white hair, while others report a darker coat and a pointed head.

ALMA
This "wild man" of Central Asia is reputedly smaller than Bigfoot and less ape-like in build. In the late 1950s, based on his research into reported sightings, Soviet scientist Boris Porshnev suggested that these "wild men" were remnant populations of Neanderthal man.

WHERE IN THE WORLD?

More than 400 reports of Bigfoot sightings come from the west-coast American states of California, Oregon and Washington, and from the Canadian province of British Columbia. Other sightings have been reported from almost every part of Canada and the USA.

DID YOU KNOW?

● Many people who have shot at Bigfoot from point-blank range report that the creature seems invulnerable to gunfire.

● In 1995, a sample of alleged Bigfoot hair was sent for DNA analysis at Ohio State University. After years of testing, the results are still inconclusive.

● Hunters claim their dogs shy away from Bigfoot, whimpering.

INDEX